BBC

DOCTOR WHO

TRAVELS IN TIME
COLORING BOOK

PSS!

PRICE STERN SLOAN

An Imprint of Penguin Random House LLC

First published in the United Kingdom in 2016 by Puffin Books. First published in the United States of America in 2016 by Price Stern Sloan, an imprint of Penguin Random House LLC, 345 Hudson Street, New York, New York 10014. *PSS!* is a registered trademark of Penguin Random House LLC. Manufactured in China.

ISBN 9780451534255 10 9 8 7 6 5 4 3 2 1

THIS BOOK BELONGS TO

Abby G.

THINGS TO FIND WITHIN TIME AND SPACE...

The Meddling Monk

Venetian mask

Cactus

Torch

Thistle

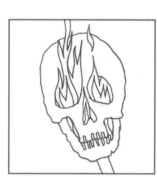

Burning skull

The Tower of London

Koh-i-noor diamond

Dalek

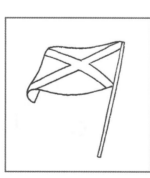

Scottish flag

Telephone

Frank Sinatra

THIS IS ONE CORNER OF ONE COUNTRY, IN ONE CONTINENT,
ON ONE PLANET, THAT'S A CORNER OF A GALAXY, THAT'S A CORNER
OF A UNIVERSE THAT IS FOREVER GROWING AND SHRINKING
AND CREATING AND DESTROYING AND NEVER REMAINING
THE SAME FOR A SINGLE MILLISECOND.

AND THERE IS SO, SO MUCH TO SEE.

Turn the page to begin a colouring adventure through time, with famous
figures and moments from throughout all of human history. Plus, of course,
a certain madman with a box . . .

13 798 000 000 BC

Letters fifty feet high. A message from the dawn of time. And no one knows what it says, because no one's ever translated it.

The Eleventh Doctor, 'The Pandorica Opens', 2010

4 600 000 000 BC

They didn't just bury something at the centre of the Earth. They became the centre of the Earth.

The Tenth Doctor, 'The Runaway Bride', 2006

140 000 000 BC

Definitely Jurassic. There's a nip in the air, though. We can't be far off the Pleistocene era.

The Fifth Doctor, 'Time-Flight', 1982

100 000 BC

If you could touch the alien sand and hear the cries of strange birds and watch them wheel in another sky, would that satisfy you?

The First Doctor, 'The Cave of Skulls', 1963

1193 BC

If I am not a god, how do you account for my supernatural knowledge?

The First Doctor, 'Temple of Secrets', 1965

64 AD

There's one thing you've got to learn about me. When I say we go to Rome, then we go to Rome. Goodnight.

The First Doctor, 'The Romans', 1965

79 AD

Just someone. Please. Not the whole town. Just save someone.

Donna Noble, 'The Fires of Pompeii', 2008

102 AD

I return to my command after one week and discover we've been playing host to Cleopatra. Who's in Egypt. And dead!

Roman Commander, 'The Pandorica Opens', 2010

102 AD

Hello, Stonehenge! Who takes the Pandorica, takes the universe!

The Eleventh Doctor, 'The Pandorica Opens', 2010

476 AD

We have reason to believe there's something rather unusual in the loch . . .

The Brigadier, 'Terror of the Zygons', 1975

800 AD

Fly like a bird, run like a nose. That's probably a Viking saying. I haven't checked that.

The Twelfth Doctor, 'The Girl Who Died', 2015

1066 AD

He loses the Battle of Hastings to William the Conqueror. Well, at least that's what the history books said happened . . .

The First Doctor, 'A Battle of Wits', 1965

1215 AD

Medieval misfits! Don't think you've won yet, Doctor . . .

The Master, 'The King's Demons', 1983

1228 AD

Long-haired ninny versus robot killer knights? I know where I'd put my money.

The Twelfth Doctor, 'Robot of Sherwood', 2014

1300 AD

I spent all day yesterday in a bow tie, the day before in a long scarf. It's my party, and all of me is invited.

The Twelfth Doctor, 'The Magician's Apprentice', 2015

1336 AD

We'd just left Raxacoricofallapatorius. Then we went to Kyoto. That's right – Japan in 1336!

The Ninth Doctor, 'Bad Wolf', 2005

1430 AD

What's the point of travelling through time and space if we can't change anything?

Barbara Wright, 'The Aztecs', 1964

1505 AD

Is that all you can say? No eyebrows? We're talking about the Mona Lisa!

The Fourth Doctor, 'City of Death', 1979

1562 AD

Tell me, Doctor, why I'm wasting my time on you. I have wars to plan.

Elizabeth I, 'The Day of the Doctor', 2013

1580 AD

One city to save an entire species. Was that so much to ask?

Rosanna Calvierri, 'The Vampires of Venice', 2010

1599 AD

It made me question everything. The futility of this fleeting existence. To be or not to be? Oh, that's quite good.

William Shakespeare, 'The Shakespeare Code', 2007

1651 AD

You gad about while I trudge through the centuries, day by day, hour by hour. Do you ever think or care what happens after you've flown away?

Me, 'The Woman Who Lived', 2015

1666 AD

I have a sneaking suspicion this fire should be allowed to run its course.

The Fifth Doctor, 'The Visitation', 1982

1699 AD

Yo-ho-ho! Or does nobody actually say that?

The Eleventh Doctor, 'The Curse of the Black Spot', 2011

1742 AD

There is a man coming to Versailles. He has watched over me my whole life and he will not desert me tonight.

Madame de Pompadour, 'The Girl in the Fireplace', 2006

1746 AD

I'm just beginning to enjoy myself. Down with King George!

The Second Doctor, 'The Highlanders', 1966

1851 AD

T - A - R - D - I - S. It stands for Tethered Aerial Release Developed in Style!

Jackson Lake, 'The Next Doctor', 2008

1869 AD

I don't wish to impose on you, but I must ask you . . . My books, Doctor. Do they last?

Charles Dickens, 'The Unquiet Dead', 2005

1870 AD

I see 'keep out' signs as suggestions more than actual orders. Like 'dry clean only'.

The Eleventh Doctor, 'A Town Called Mercy', 2012

1879 AD

You want weapons? We're in a library! Books! The best weapons in the world!

The Tenth Doctor, 'Tooth and Claw', 2006

1890 AD

You see how they roar their light. Everywhere we look, the complex magic of nature blazes before our eyes.

Vincent Van Gogh, 'Vincent and the Doctor', 2010

1892 AD

Run. Run, you clever boy, and remember.

Clara Oswald, 'The Snowmen', 2012

1913 AD

He's ancient and forever. He burns at the centre of time and can see the turn of the universe. And . . . he's wonderful.

Tim Latimer, 'The Family of Blood', 2007

1926 AD

Turns out we are in the middle of a murder mystery. One of yours, Dame Agatha.

The Tenth Doctor, 'The Unicorn and the Wasp', 2008

1930 AD

I've always wanted to go to New York. I mean the real New York, not the new, new, new, new, new one.

Martha Jones, 'Daleks in Manhattan', 2007

1935 AD

I don't like it. There's something happening on this mountain. I can feel it.

The Second Doctor, 'The Abominable Snowmen', 1967

1941 AD

You're amazing, the lot of you. Don't know what you do to Hitler, but you frighten the hell out of me.

The Ninth Doctor, 'The Empty Child', 2005

1941 AD

Think of what I could achieve with your remarkable machine, Doctor. The lives that could be saved.

Winston Churchill, 'Victory of the Daleks', 2010

1952 AD

Guys, we've really got to go quite quickly. I just accidentally got engaged to Marilyn Monroe.

The Eleventh Doctor, 'A Christmas Carol', 2010

1953 AD

Kick off your shoes and enjoy the coronation. Believe me, you'll be glued to the screen.

The Wire, 'The Idiot's Lantern', 2006

1969 AD

That's an astronaut. That's an Apollo astronaut, in a lake.

Rory Williams, 'The Impossible Astronaut', 2011

1983 AD

Hair, shoulder pads, nukes. It's the 1980s. Everything's bigger.

The Eleventh Doctor, 'Cold War', 2013

1987 AD

Peter Alan Tyler, my dad. The most wonderful man in the world. Died the seventh of November, 1987.

Rose Tyler, 'Father's Day', 2005

2006 AD

Nine hundred years of time and space, and I've never been slapped by someone's mother.

The Ninth Doctor, 'Aliens of London', 2005

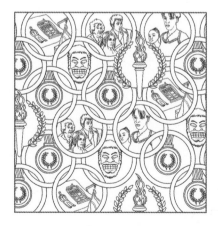

2012 AD

Tonight they'll light the Olympic flame in the stadium, and the whole world will be looking at our city.

Trish Webber, 'Fear Her', 2006